After The War Comes Love
Volume 1

Sophie Cloud

After The War Comes Love
Volume 1

Olympia Publishers
London

www.olympiapublishers.com
OLYMPIA PAPERBACK EDITION

A CIP catalogue record for this title is
available from the British Library.

ISBN: 978-1-78830-495-5

First Published in 2020

Olympia Publishers
Tallis House
2 Tallis Street
London
EC4Y 0AB

Printed in Great Britain

Acknowledgements

For Barnes, as always. Also, to my favourite Poets –
Geoffrey Chaucer, Lord Byron and Rupert Brooke. And
to my Muse.

A Beat to the Drum

The Orange Lilies they lay bare,
to trump call their Master's mare.
Sound the drums, pomp and ceremony,
over the brow, thou have gone,
not to return to me.

The horse lay, braying and swaying.
Look to the South, the surrender has come.
Too late for some, our boys their resting place,
on foreign lands, and drums proud, and now,
silenced to the beat.

The land swells with brown soil,
risen where green once lay hidden.
Here I lay my mighty sword,
and cut the cord of all heartache.

The mothers, without them now,
as day breaks, their sons will not be with them.
Their lives forthright,
beat a humdrum existence,
a numbness to the time,
of all encompassing war.

My Lily

You will not wither whilst I am away.
My Lily,
as lilies of the field do not.
They grow, they do not toil too long and neither do they spin,
so stay upright and proud.
Do not bend in these hard times of ours.
Lilies bring you beauty, colour and fragrance.
My hardy fleur.
We cannot become like a weed and be cut down like her.
So we too need a little care,
to be beautiful and long-lived.
Do not bend in these hard times of ours.

Emmeline

Born Moss Side,
she went on a political ride.
Free thinking, without blinkers,
her advocacy of women's rights.
Ribbons of green, purple and white,
she wore,
representing women's awareness of their plight,
to fight the good fight.

Voice of reform in the workhouse,
she was never a timid mouse.
She gave care to the aid of single mums,
whose fathers were on the front line.
Women's empowerment,
she never ceased to retire,
with an excuse or a pardon of fruits of her labour,
to a statue in Victoria Garden.

(Emmeline Pankhurst) 1858–1928

Metal on Metal

An indigo flare lights up the sky without warning,
across the bay a person is in mourning.
The softening, quickening of the distress of my heart,
is the sailor's dilemma more painful to part,
than my untwisting, slowly healing soul?

Gathering momentum as time moves on,
I hear the seagulls screeching song.
Metal on metal against the elements,
am I still a man of no sentiments?

Left to build another life,
to be reunited with others from my past,
all because they cling to this mast,
of steel and varnish,
and things that shine,
and bring to me such hostility.

Cowboy Boots

Cowboy boots,
on weathered land.
I miss the wet damp soil of England.
Brown boots,
are what I remember,
on French clay soil.
On England's cobbled streets,
my shiny brogues on theatre land.
I wish to be barefooted now,
aloft in the skies.
My feet too well travelled,
and too well trod.

(Bertram Wright returning from flying. Poem from Orange
Lilies of Dallington Place)

Love is Different
The Black Panther and the Cockatoo
Part 1

I'm slinking about.
I'm looking at you,
you have tamed me dear one.
I look into your eyes.
I know I am your pet.

I can do no harm,
I will come to you.
By your feet and lie for a while.
I will go away,
and you will forget me for a while.
But do not worry about me.
And I will be back.

Back to say hello,
and stare into your eyes,
with deep admiration.
I am yours.
You are mine,
but we don't hold each other.

A Peaceful Soldier

Walk upon sharp pebbles for me,
then I will know your love.
Suffer, your knees,
get down and proud,
then I will know your love.

Make way for a hero,
Lion or Lioness,
to brace to free one's motives to confess.

Yet to the people,
who slay the dragons,
they are not the only brave.
Ones that walk in peace,
a hundred years on,
on and on,
are those that will make this battle cease.

Love

Love, love, love.
Could you pass me that, Love!

Come hither, Love,
or how are you Love?

It may sound derogatory,
but it is still love.

Should we complain?
When we are sharing love?

You decide... Love.

Red Autumn

Across from the Castle and down from the glen.
Red fire and burnished gold,
settles the mist,
quickly and ghostly.

Ruby red, the setter strides,
alongside his master he glides.
Past scarlet tartan, and berried folk,
by battlements of stone blood soaked.

Mottled red are his fingertips,
ripped by the heat,
the dog busies his sniffing nose through the peat.
His fur like silky burgundy wine.
An ever faithful guide, his master's canine.

Up the steep slope, from russet clay to grey.
There from the tower, a view of the season.
An autumn so rare, so majestic, without reason,
to be honest, the warmest October it is.
Stand still and feel our weather,
a clement excuse for an almost treason.

Skinny Dipping with Rupert
(Rupert Brooke and Virginia Woolf)

Whilst staying with Rita,
(you should meet her),
we played a game you see.
If one loved another,
we would challenge each other,
to skinny dip at Longthornton Manor.

The moon now in its glamorous form,
ready to reveal the figures that swim,
silhouettes exposed, Virginia disposed,
and captivated by her lover.

For he in love with someone else,
swam faster, and firmer away from her grip.
Virginia, a married lady of course,
but couldn't resist the obsession for Rupert.

She swam better than anyone else I knew,
and Rupert flattered by such a talented,
and exhorted lady,
let her catch up with him or did he?
That's what Virginia told me.

Take Flight in the Black Sheriff

There were sixty-eight of us, now forty-two.
The last left behind us, so we can forge ahead.
Some injured, some dead,
my friends, my comrades,
with tales left unsaid.
I will write for them,
the tales I know and have witnessed.
A ghastly mix of loss and sadness, of scenes obscene,
lives snuffed out.
Men with such a vigour, youth, a wasted oblivion.
I gulp down life and rise about the clouds.
Listing men and actions,
some proud and some mundane.
No one else will tell their story as I climb and soar,
a hundred feet,
to win and sometime fold to defeat.
A hard landing for us all.
The plane judders safely back to land.
My lungs expand to the fear and cries,
where we go and where we demise.
But I will rise and not fail.
I will not finish my life,
here in France's clay soiled land.
A handful, a mighty handful of England's grace,
will return, at last to their loves,
and vows to their country,
God speed.

The Wild Rock Rose

What are you tonight?
Surprise me.
Lie to me,
but still love me.

Tease me.
Please me.
Lie to me,
still love me.

But leather clad,
you were always the cad,
but lie to me,
I'll take it,
but still love me.

Wild rogue are you,
stillness is not your thing.
As you roam,
lie to me,
try to be,
but still I love you.

Surpass me by.
Surprise me again.
You leave, no reprieve,
but lie to me once more,
and I am gone.

Canto of a Bloody War Part 1 England 1916

The breeze brings with it an air of glory,
only hanging by a tumultuous onslaught
of fear.
Our nerves serve their time on the edge,
dangling over the precipice of this war,
to victory or loss.

A young factory girl slouches over sacking.
The dim light now finding as she gathers her skirts.
Clocking out and switching off the light.
A humming sound to be heard overhead.

Her breath quickening,
her heart upwards to her lips.
Seeming to leap out of her chest
and out.
Can anyone see it beating by a quiet
close, a village green?

The monster ticks on,
a travelling ghost.
Ghostly against the silver moon,
her lover meets her at the gate,
as they dash through hidden wood,
heads down and out of sight.

They are alive today,
safe in each other's arms,
some not so lucky.
As the silver bullet reaches over London.
Red fire lights up the south,
closing eyes as if to make it disappear.
It does so, back to the enemy.

Sailing Ship

I heard a whisper in my sleep.
Thoughts and riddles that do keep.
Locked tight in slumber memories,
I still remember you.

Whispers slip under door,
of transoceanic shore.
That face so clear, I wonder how you are.

Children's plays as curtain falls,
weeping, screaming, animosity rules.
Happy times with peace of mind.
How these days did quickly grind.

With every sunbeam,
I think of you.
Laughing, smiling face,
but now has gone without a trace.
But do not forget,
I think of that tall Sailing Ship,
that takes me on to you on every trip.

So leave a light on for me when I'm not here.
This you will do and please do swear.
I'll be here, if not now,
watching you from the bow.
Please keep it burning,
and I will see,
the things that were special,
of you and me.

Gleaming face and teary eye,
your cat-like legs,
running against the tide.
I'm hoping that this will keep you happy,
my sweet dear friend of mine.

I love you with my soul,
every part is for you.
So feel my presence,
whilst I'm away,
and I will do the same,
so keep it burning for yonder day.

Third Floor Flat

Up in the third floor flat
she paces up and down
round and around.

Head is spinning,
gloved hands are a twitching.
'What to do?' 'What to do?' she cries
amidst the steam and 'Whicker's World'.

The potatoes are boiling
the sun is shining
but her heart is crying
up in the third floor flat.

She is old yet young.
How old does she look so far away?
Body stooped low,
hair a shade of grey,
nobody cares anyway
up in the third floor flat.

Embellish me Not for I am Flawed

Embellish me not,
for I am flaw'd.
I have clawed my way back from Hell's own fire,
where I was left to quench my own cheapest desire.
I am Joseph, a simple man, love me as I am.

The sea divides with time in mind,
my life as it is now split in two.
The waves of grief against the shores of my old,
anonymous soul.
I, Joseph, a man to be judged,
whose faulted images to aspire,
to something I do not recognise.
I am loved when I am bereft,
am loathed when I am full.

Age makes sense of this euphemism,
for I am Joseph, a lost man,
and one who is eventually found, by you.

(J. Handley to his wife, Mai)

Willow Tree
From the Orange Lilies of Dallington Place

Encase me in the Willow,
for I will not weep.
Judge me by the billow,
so not to keep.
Open your arms,
and let me walk amongst the spaces.
Do not fold your branches,
so thin are the traces.
I can disperse, in a fair swoop,
as the wind blows; I will return.
A spore is let loose,
I am more than before.
Each particle travels,
not sure where to land.
Unravel sweet Catkin,
forty seeds venture forth,
lost in a myriad,
of openness and kind.
Where do you go,
what do you find?
To seek your growth,
you cannot be pinned.
Each North, South, East and West.
Lovely resting place; forlorn but free.
A soft landing, a mating mound,
A quiet spot, a lofty croft.
A meadow, a stream,

a bird, a scene,
it doesn't make the difference,
of places, time, or sight.
Rights are abound,
Everything goes to ground
a branch and tree;
Weeping Willow encase me,
test me, and I will revolt,
a horse, a wild gripping colt.
A spirit of life that cannot be withheld,
felled me,
and you will know every length of your leaves,
will shed a tear;
It is right when the storm takes,
you will bend, but will not break.
Be open, and then closed;
the only way to be, is flexible with me.

Blackfriars Bridge   1986

That day we talked for hours.
And as I walked across Blackfriars Bridge,
I remember the past, the future and in between.

And down towards the tunnel, I crossed,
in between, looking behind and then forward,
wondering what would be seen.

The tramp's clothing, drawing the equator,
of past and future, and no sign of him,
but for a sweaty cap and a can of lager.

I ran faster and faster not knowing,
how safe I would be this side of life.
The tube awaits, bringing me forward towards,
the future, of happiness, grief and sorrow.
But here I am looking forward to tomorrow.

Two Lovers

We two are lovers,
split in two by verging waves,
gathering great their power of life.
The moon's opaqueness views their strife.
The lovers under one lair.

You willowy beauty,
you astral wildcat,
gravity skims your outer skin.
I am that jaundiced fellow chasing his tigress
for reason,
to level thee to stay with me,
and float you down my river of sweet notes, my nightingale.

Only when we are one,
can we be lovers eternally.
To seek a peaceful horizon,
beyond your fears.
Oils and blossoms parallel the misty blue,
to lie with levity,
as I will with you.

A Summer Song

A Summer song,
a longing, a gaze, a phrase,
that reminds me,
of the languishing days,
in the hot Summer maze.

I found you by the cove,
lying there,
a sweat, a teardrop, a sleep,
to keep a photo of your slumber.
You said you had my number.

After Summer days had gone,
I couldn't hear the song.
You didn't call, no chirp,
no tweet, a silence too discreet.
Where had it gone, that Summer song?

A memory of our walk along the promenade.
Your feet I remember were sore,
as the sand rubbed between your toes.
I held your sandals for you,
as I listened to your woes,
in the last of those Summer days.

The day we said goodbye,
I held you to my breast.
You said we had the Winter,
and everything and the rest.
But I haven't heard a cheep,
a bleep, or a conversation to sleep.
The Summer days have gone,
There is now no Summer song.

The Ghost of Abbeville

Click down on this earth beyond,
your rifle lays in the mud.
Catch a light,
a ciggie bright,
to keep the cold at bay.

Click down,
I see you frown.
You know we won't make morning.
All seeing face crack in disgrace,
your loyalty has me again.

Click down there on the road home,
I without you.
I am afraid of the turn in the road.
I am alone, and without you,
I will be scorned.
I came back without you.

Click down, am I alive?
My fingers burn brightly in the mist.
Click down.
I hear you. What does the census say?
I am one soldier listed,
perished at Abbeville.